# Picking the Low-Hanging Fruit
...and Other Stupid Stuff We Say In the Corporate World

by James Sudakow
illustrated by Todd Kale

VOLUME 1

PURPLE
SQUIRREL
MEDIA GROUP

Picking the Low-Hanging Fruit

James Sudakow

Copyright © 2016 by James Sudakow

Illustrations copyright © 2016 by Todd Kale

Purple Squirrel Media
San Diego, California
www.purplesquirrelmedia.net

Print ISBN: 978-0-9965033-1-0

Electronic ISBN: 978-0-9965033-0-3

*Thanks to all of the corporate irreverents I have met and befriended through the years. Laughing alongside you all at the preposterous expressions that were hurled around the corporate world with reckless abandon ultimately inspired this book.*

*And for all those who toil in cubicles, lost and confused, may this shine a light—even if that light is a bit dim.*

# Table of Contents

*No one wanted to admit they had not understood anything the project lead had just said.*

# What is this gibberish?

Sitting in one of my first project team meetings of my first professional job after college, I listened intently to our project leader give us our directions:

"We need to quickly put a SWAT team together to come up with some good thoughtware and really map out a straw dog for this deliverable. Then I'll ask you all to put some flesh on the bones and drill down into this. Do not keep this at the 20,000-foot level. At the end of the day, we've got to prepare a deck and demonstrate that we're all singing from the same song sheet while also dovetailing with the critical path deliverables that Stern's team is currently vectoring towards. I'm going to be out of pocket, so I'd like to have DeArmen lead this work thread. It's really in his bailiwick, and I'm not going to have the bandwidth. We may not have the critical mass to actually operationalize this, so let's make sure that we do the appropriate data dump with the key stakeholders. Lastly, let's make these deliverables really robust enough to drive towards a significant paradigm shift so that this deck representing our work doesn't become shelfware. Any questions?"

Thoughtware? Straw dogs? Singing from the same song sheet? What did all of this mean? I sat with my colleagues presenting my best poker face, trying not to let it become obvious that I had understood none of the instructions we had just been given. Had I missed something in school? Why wasn't a class covering these terms included in the languages or sociology section of my college curriculum? I reflected on what I thought had been a good education, which was supposed to have prepared me for the corporate world. I had earned a college degree with a good GPA from a good school. Like most, I had partaken in many typical college extracurricular activities—most of which seemed to have involved consuming large quantities of beer in short quantities of time. Whereas I was pretty sure that these activities had resulted in reducing my number of working brain cells, I still felt as though I had walked out relatively unscathed. I then went out and got myself a nice graduate degree and continued my learning experience with less focus on beer consumption.

By the time I was done, I had learned about a lot of things—stuff like corporate strategy, basic and even some moderately advanced accounting and finance, marketing, operations, human resources, and IT. I knew about fancy things like the double-entry system of accounting, accruals, amortization, mergers and acquisitions, economies of scale, zero-based budgeting, organizational design, and systems implementations methodologies. I had even acquired some foundational internship experiences prior to officially entering the "real world." Admittedly, my role in those unpaid internships was limited to mastering the very nonstrategic and hardly glamorous role of making copies for everyone and successfully creating glorious looking PowerPoint presentations. I knew that I still had much to learn but felt confident that I could make a meaningful contribution to whatever company I chose and that chose me. I wasn't so sure anymore.

Over the years, though, I adapted. I had to. I was hearing these expressions lobbed in my general direction on a daily basis. But adaptation had its unexpected consequences. By the time that I was ten years into my career, I found that I was actually using many of these ridiculous expressions and not thinking twice about it anymore. Just what had they been serving me in the company cafeteria all these years anyway? It seemed as though I had drunk the Kool-Aid and had slowly succumbed to a Jim Jones-like corporate cult cleverly disguised in business casual attire. I realized that I needed deprogramming the day I suggested to one of my close friends, who did not work in the corporate world, "Let's map out a plan of action" just to decide which Sunday football game to watch. Some sort of dramatic intervention was needed. If I didn't take immediate action, I might end up using these expressions on dates and would never meet a woman who wanted to hang out with me for any extended period of time.

The next day I devised a plan. On the wall in my office was a whiteboard, presumably placed there for me to use for important work-like endeavors, probably to "map things out." Not anymore. On the whiteboard, I listed all of the terms that my coworkers (and boldly even my superiors) were not allowed to use in my office. I then let my colleagues know that if they absolutely could not control themselves from using any of the terms on the whiteboard, they were required to use air quotes with their fingers.

This might just embarrass everyone enough to change their behavior.

Unfortunately, the little experiment proved to do absolutely nothing to inhibit anyone from using these expressions. To my surprise, though, my colleagues adhered without any resistance whatsoever to the air-quoting requirement, which at times got distracting due to the sheer volume of finger bending occurring in my office. Somehow, they all seemed to enjoy the fact that they were required to do this. And the list on my whiteboard mysteriously grew longer. Within a very short period of time, I discovered that I wasn't the only one adding words to the board. My fellow coworkers began to sneak into my office and add words to the whiteboard themselves. I would return from meetings and business trips only to find new words squeezed in wherever there was blank space—sideways, in tiny print, and in small corners. Then when I would encounter my colleagues in the halls, those responsible would proudly take credit for the words they had added. But if we all knew how ridiculous we sounded using these expressions and were even willing to do funny things with our fingers when we talked, why did we continue to use these terms? Sadly, my experiment didn't make a dent in solving that conundrum.

So as the expression goes: "If you can't beat them, join them." Or as they might say in the corporate world: "If you can't create a win-win proposition, effectively gain traction, and socialize your burning platform for a paradigm shift, bake yourself into the current process." And that is the genesis of this book. Whereas at some point in my life I aspire to do something that creates positive social impact in the world, this book is not that thing. This book is merely an attempt to help people in the corporate world figure out what everyone around them is actually talking about. And since I can't make any of you use air quotes when you read it, I can at least throw in a few jokes along the way. But let me be upfront: I claim no creative license for having invented any of the terms or expressions you will read about in this book. For an expression to be included here, I had to have heard it to the point where I started to dream about it. Maybe one day we can all stop using these expressions and speak English again. Until then, I hope this book helps you decipher what your coworkers are saying.

*At the end of the day*

# At the end of the day

## *What does this mean?*

The point when a project milestone or the project itself is completed, leading to an important outcome needed from the work

## *What this doesn't mean:*

At the end of *today*

## *How is this used in a sentence?*

"At the end of the day, we are going to have to show significant improvement in process turnaround time, or we will lose credibility with our customers."

## *More information:*

Take solace in the fact that "at the end of the day" almost never means at the end of the current day. If someone who works at your company needs something from you by the end of today, you will definitely know. He or she will likely ask you approximately every twelve minutes if you've finished yet, making it all the more difficult to finish.

*Bake that (or him/her) into the process*

# Bake that (or him/her) into the process

## What does this mean?

Include it (or him/her)

## What this doesn't mean:

Anything at all is being baked anywhere nearby, including the company cafeteria. Don't go get your oven mitts. We won't be making the homemade seven-layer cake that Phil from Accounts Receivable made famous at last year's company holiday party.

## How is this used in a sentence?

Employee #1: "Can we make sure that we get a very clear picture of the systems integration requirements?"

Employee #2: "Yes, we will absolutely make sure to bake that into the process."

## More information:

Very frequently, people will be baked into a process too. Baking is not just for things or information. As strange and sadistic as it may sound to suggest that we will bake David into the work, just remember that David will not meet an untimely death in the kitchen of the company cafeteria.

# Bandwidth

### *What does this mean?*

Time and/or resources needed to meet a project requirement or deadline

### *What this doesn't mean:*

We're doing power band training as part of our wellness program. Initially, Ken from Finance scoffed at this workout as too remedial given his self-proclaimed athletic prowess. But he seems to be changing his perspective after somehow managing to yet again entangle himself in the pink and blue bands. He's currently lying on the ground in the atrium and is in dire need of help if he is going to make the budget reconciliation meeting in 15 minutes.

### *How is this used in a sentence?*

"I just don't have the bandwidth to get these new objectives completed in the time frame you've outlined. I'd delegate this down to my team, but nobody on my team has the bandwidth either. They just picked up an additional project from Ken's team due to that team's resource constraints after Ken had to be rushed to the Urgent Care center."

### *More information:*

Given that the balance between the work required in the corporate world and the resources allocated to do the work is frequently teetering on the edge of what is reasonable, employees very frequently refer to a lack of bandwidth. From time to time, eager, upwardly focused employees, who will never admit to not having enough bandwidth, will take on everything as a way of moving up in the company. Though admirable, these employees are often quickly buried by all of the work that their coworkers immediately off-load onto them as if part of a fire sale.

# Bench strength

### What does this mean?

The amount of depth we have in the organization for specific knowledge and capabilities. Bench strength is often expressed in terms of the number of employees with critical knowledge or skills as well as the depth of knowledge and experience possessed by those employees.

### What this doesn't mean:

Anything at all related to the structure and strength of the benches in the front lobby. We have just had them reinforced after the recent unfortunate incident in which the CEO from one of our key accounts had an embarrassing encounter with what he has now infamously labeled as our "man-eating chairs."

After really asserting his power position and laying into Rina in the finance meeting before lunch, Ken found himself suddenly nervous when he then saw Rina bench-pressing two hundred pounds in the company fitness center during a lunchtime workout.

### How is this used in a sentence?

"We just don't have the internal bench strength to develop this new technology in house."

### More information:

Almost all organizations experience some challenges around having the bench strength needed to deliver on all of the company's goals and objectives, leading to the always difficult question: Build bench strength so we can do it ourselves? Or hire consultants to do it? If you are looking for answers to these strategic questions, you'll have to read another book—one that will likely have far fewer cartoon illustrations.

"Our project data needs to be organized into appropriate buckets so we can develop our recommendations."

# Buckets

### What does this mean?

Groups of data or information that fit together

### What this doesn't mean:

Go put the buckets out around the perimeter of the building. The storm drains are not working well, and we're in for a heavy downpour later today.

### How is this used in a sentence?

"We'll need to take all of the data we've gathered during the assessment phase and put it into appropriate buckets so we can develop our recommendations."

### More information:

When people in the corporate world start talking about buckets, usually a lot of data needs to be organized. As a result, someone will inevitably be assigned to be the organizer of the data. Whereas this is not an entirely bad task to be assigned, often others in the organization have made a predetermination of what the buckets will be. This premature bucket development makes the task of putting data into buckets difficult because frequently the data does not logically fit into any of these predetermined buckets. Good luck.

Also, some people in the corporate world have attempted to turn this term into a verb as follows: "We will need to 'bucketize' the data." Don't take this as an opportunity to remind them that their seventh grade English teacher would be very disappointed in their lack of grammatical rigor.

*Build a straw man*

# Build a straw man / Build a straw dog

## *What does this mean?*

Make an outline

## *What this doesn't mean:*

We're building a scarecrow to place strategically in the company parking lot. Everyone is getting really tired of those bird droppings all over our cars.

We're making a straw dog companion for the straw man scarecrow we just erected in the parking lot.

## *How is this used in a sentence?*

"Let's build a straw man and show it to senior leadership before we get too far into the details. If they are not comfortable with this, we can scrap it and create another one."

But not...

"Whose turn is it to take the straw dog out for a straw walk? He's chewing on Lisa's cube again. Why did we build a straw puppy again?"

## *More information:*

When you hear this term, don't go out and get some straw. More importantly, don't waste valuable time working on anything in detail. Straw men change all the time, mostly because the top-level leaders asking for the straw men often don't know what they are looking for until they see it, which typically requires much painful iteration.

Also note that "straw man" and "straw dog" can be used interchangeably. But it is important to understand that there is no such thing as a "straw woman", even if you are admirably suggesting that the straw man might get lonely without a straw woman companion. Equally importantly, dogs are the only animal that can be substituted for a straw man. Straw cats, straw hamsters, and straw chinchillas are not acceptable in the corporate world even though they all, like dogs, make fabulous domesticated pets.

*Build a straw dog*

# Burning platform

### What does this mean?

Something within the company that needs to be addressed quickly or else the company will suffer significantly; a highly compelling call to action

### What this doesn't mean:

Go get the fire extinguisher, call 911, and evacuate! This is not a drill. For your own safety, you might not want to remain inside like you did during last month's drill, when you decided that it was more important to finish your department fantasy football draft (you know who you are Accounting department).

### How is this used in a sentence?

"For this initiative to be successful, we really need to make the case for change. If not, leadership will just ask us, 'What's the burning platform? Why do we need to do this?'"

### More information:

When presenting your burning platform, make sure that it is truly a raging inferno and not merely a smoldering fire pit ready to burn out. Understand that if you have to think too hard to come up with the burning platform for your initiative, maybe there really isn't a need for the project in the first place, and the company can focus time on the other 832 initiatives that have been deemed as the most critical priorities.

*Note:* Do not assume that other corporate terms referencing fire (such as "firefighting" and "putting out fires") have anything at all to do with burning platforms. These terms are completely unrelated even though logic might dictate otherwise. "Firefighting" and "putting out fires" both refer to the need for employees and managers to reactively solve continuous problems emerging every day. These are different kinds of fires than the burning platform. You want the platform on fire. Understand that if you fire fight the burning platform, you will upset many of your coworkers who have worked very hard to get the platform on fire in the first place.

*Change agent*

# Change agent

## *What does this mean?*

A person formally or informally responsible for influencing change in the company

## *What this doesn't mean:*

Your work is anything at all like what agents do in the FBI or CIA.

You have top secret information on your company's special ops.

You always seem to have a lot of loose change. People come to you for help at the vending machine.

## *How is this used in a sentence?*

"For this project to be successful, we really need to select some strong change agents who can influence effectively in their respective functions."

## *More information:*

If you have been identified as a change agent, recognize that you are viewed positively as someone who can effectively influence your coworkers as well as someone who is open to change. Also recognize that almost everyone else in your company fears change more than a visit to the dentist for a long, deep root canal. Your job as a change agent will often feel like trying to push a rope up a hill while coworkers angrily hurl office supplies at your head.

"Hey, Diane, how would you like to join my change network?
Not to be brash, but all of the cool people from Accounts
Receivable are trying to get in on this."

# Change network

## *What does this mean?*

A formal infrastructure comprised of carefully selected people to help manage how we are going to make changes of any kind happen successfully in an organization—in other words, a cohort of influential people we need to involve to help us make the change

## *What this doesn't mean:*

Too many people are watching celebrity gossip programming in the break room and not getting their work done. Walter from HR had a brilliant suggestion to change the network to CSPAN—the only network that might make reconciling that 935 line spreadsheet seem interesting and even exciting by comparison.

## *How is this used in a sentence?*

"We need to set up a change network that stretches across all of the different functions."

## *More information:*

"Change network" in the corporate dialect is a noun. The expression has no resemblance to the drunk guy in your freshman dorm room pointing at the television muttering "change (the) network."

*Create a parking lot*

# Create a parking lot

### What does this mean?

Creating a list of ideas proposed during a meeting or brainstorming session that either are off focus from the conversation topic or may not be highly valuable, thus allowing the facilitator to address them later and not disrupt the direction of the current discussion

### What this doesn't mean:

At first, Wayne thought the request to move his desk into the parking lot to manage the facilities project was demeaning. But he soon grew to like his new location when, upon measurement, he learned that parking spot 732, where his desk now sat, was actually bigger than his old office.

### How is this used in a sentence?

"Bob, that's a really interesting idea. I'd like to create a parking lot for ideas like that, which we can review later. Thank you for the good input, but let's focus on ideas to solve our accounts payable issues."

### More information:

Who is likely to say this? Anyone facilitating a working session, meeting, or brainstorming session.

Creating a parking lot is really important in the corporate world because off-topic or low-value ideas can derail any constructive discussion. If you are a facilitator, you will always want to let the group know at the beginning of the meeting that you will be creating a parking lot as a place to put these ideas.

If you are a participant in a meeting and hear your facilitator use this expression, hope that it is not your idea that has just been put in the parking lot. If it is, you need to be realistic and understand that the idea you've proposed isn't considered to be very good at all or your idea was completely unrelated to anything anyone was talking about. Nobody wanted to discourage your participation in the meeting, so you have been put in the parking lot. Just understand that there is a very good chance that your idea *will never be discussed again.*

# Critical mass

### What does this mean?

A large enough quantity of resources, including people, that will either allow the required work to be completed effectively or ensure that a significant change is enacted

### What this doesn't mean:

Anything to do with the weight-loss club that the Communications department started after the holidays

### How is this used in a sentence?

"We just don't seem to have the critical mass of people with the skill set to manage this systems upgrade."

Please not...

"I'm going to reach a critical mass that will require me to buy new pants if Frank keeps bringing donuts to our daily huddle meeting."

# Cross-pollination

## What does this mean?

Creating opportunities for employees to gain different experiences, exposure, and knowledge by exchanging them into different functions or teams or by sharing information across projects for mutual benefit

## What this doesn't mean:

Anything to do with bees, pollen, or botany

Everyone but Lori knew why she had been written up for creating an uncomfortable employee relations issue after Darryl claimed that she had used a strange and inappropriate pickup line with him after the systems implementation planning meeting. "She said that she had noticed me looking at her in the conference room just now and asked me if I wanted to cross-pollinate after work. I wasn't even sure what this meant but still kind of felt a little violated," Darryl said meekly in his discussion with Human Resources.

## How is this used in a sentence?

"For part of our overall employee development planning, we should identify ways to create opportunities for cross-pollination across the different groups."

*Data dump*

# Data dump

### What does this mean?

A huge amount of information given to a new employee or project member. The intention of the data dump is to bring the new team member up to date on the project and enable him or her to be ready to contribute quickly.

### What this doesn't mean:

We're staying late tonight to destroy incriminating data from the Bridgeport account; we'll be dumping it into our competitor's trash bins at 3:00 a.m.

### How is this used in a sentence?

"Let's set up a time next week to do a data dump for the two new team members."

### More information:

If you are the one who will be receiving the data dump, be prepared to receive at least 23 e-mails with 7 attachments on each e-mail. The processing speed of your computer will be reduced to a fast crawl because at least one of the files is so large that it will clog your network. If the data dumper suspects in advance that this will be a problem, you will likely receive either a flash drive containing 14 zip files with 32 documents in each file or a link to some sort of SharePoint site with 65 folders and 935 files that has no sort of understandable organization scheme. You will have approximately not enough time to read through all of this and formulate any and all questions to be asked during a single Q&A session with the person/persons who will be administering the data dump and who are simultaneously trying to run away from this project as quickly as possible. You will then be on your own and expected to know everything about the project, as though you have been working on it from its inception six months ago.

*Note:* The expression "knowledge transfer" is essentially synonymous with "data dump" but suggests a kinder, gentler, more elongated process to ensure better results. Don't be fooled or caught off guard. Even in this approach, an information tsunami is coming your way. Seeking higher ground by climbing to the top of the file cabinets won't help you.

*Dead on*

# Dead on

*What does this mean?*

Exactly right

*What this doesn't mean:*

Randy knew that Bill's continuously high stress level, combined with his less-than-healthy daily diet consisting of donuts, coffee, and cheesesteak sandwiches, made him a ticking time bomb for yet another heart attack. So Randy wasn't about to take any chances, knowing that at any moment Bill could finally go. He quietly asked Justin to start prepping to take Bill's place presenting at the board of directors meeting next week.

*How is this used in a sentence?*

"Brian, your analysis of this product's problems is dead on."

*More information:*

Despite the fact that the word "dead" is in the expression, being told that you are dead on is a good thing.

# Deep dive

### What does this mean?

Detailed analysis of a very specific subject, project, or area

### What this doesn't mean:

This year's company picnic will include a diving competition. Olympic rules enforced. Minimize your splash upon water entry because the judges will be really focusing on this and making point deductions. The judge from Manufacturing—who just got his Black Belt Six Sigma certification—is particularly unrelenting on this rule.

We're going scuba diving as a team building activity.

### How is this used in a sentence?

"I think we've been able to get a pretty good understanding of what went well and what didn't go well on our initiatives this year, but I'd like for us to take a deep dive into the project that had the most milestone delays to see what more we can learn."

### More information:

Deep dives are intended to uncover every detail in a given project so that leaders can learn something from what is uncovered. Often, leaders determine the strategic need for a deep dive when something hasn't gone well or if they feel that something important is missing.

Upon confirmation that a deep dive will indeed occur, a unique team will emerge out of the corporate primordial ooze. The team will be comprised of the most anal-retentive, excruciatingly detail-oriented, meticulous employees who all somehow enjoy the task of analyzing how many minutes were spent by the project team on a daily basis reserving conference rooms. Get ready to be mired in a level of detail you may not have ever thought humanly possible (unless you work in Accounting). It will probably hurt a little.

# Deliverables

### What does this mean?

Results, final product, or project outcomes

### What this doesn't mean:

Ken was not amused by the five supreme pizzas delivered to his office every hour on the hour in response to his stern mandate that morning that his team regularly send him deliverables throughout the course of the day.

### How is this used in a sentence?

"We've got a long list of deliverables on this project, and we need to ensure that we meet every one of them in the timelines we've outlined."

### More information:

Many people in the corporate world cling to this word as if it were an old blanket from their childhoods. So don't make the mistake of thinking that you can just substitute normal words like "results" or "outcomes" in place of "deliverables" or launch minor protests by refusing to use the term. All of these have been attempted by others in the corporate world, only to be met with confusion, and a surprising amount of anger in some cases.

*"That focus group topic will dovetail nicely with our planned leadership discussion at the sales conference."*

# Dovetail

### What does this mean?

Link, connect, or integrate well (usually with another idea or concept)

### What this doesn't mean:

We've all been under a lot of stress. Tomorrow morning, instead of our usual daily huddle meeting, we're going bird-watching in the company atrium. This should put us in a more relaxed state of mind for the rest of the day.

### How is this used in a sentence?

"That focus group topic will dovetail nicely with our planned leadership discussion at the sales conference."

### More information:

There is much talk in the corporate world of integration, in all likelihood because things that should be integrated frequently seem to be separated by the likes of the Great Wall of China. Because of this, you will have a lot of opportunities to talk about how things dovetail together.

Whereas most of us in the corporate world are far too busy trying to meet unrealistic deadlines to spend any time researching the origins of this expression, I hope that someone finds some time to get to the bottom of how this became used in the business world. I did my part and took it upon myself to watch an *Animal Planet* feature on birds to see if there was any insight to be gained from nature. It seems as though the dove's tail connects in an interwoven way with itself. Whereas this is completely dissatisfying in resolving the "dovetail" expression origins, in that same segment I was fascinated to learn that an eagle can reputedly sight its prey from as far as two miles away.

*Drill down*

# Drill down

### What does this mean?

Identify the details—every single last one of them—about something (such as a project or process) that up until now has only been discussed in generality

### What this doesn't mean:

Go to the hardware store and buy a drill. As part of earthquake preparedness, we are all being required to drill everything in our cubicles to the cubicle walls.

### How is this used in a sentence?

"That's a good big-picture idea of what we need to do, but we really need to drill down into that, or we won't be able to determine how long this project will take or what our resource requirements will be. The devil is in the details."

### More information:

"Double clicking down" has the same meaning as "drill down" but is the term of choice when working in the high-tech industry (presumably related to double clicking a mouse and therefore being high-tech simply by referencing a computer accessory). Often professionals in the high-tech industry feel the need to create their own special set of esoteric expressions and terms to differentiate themselves from the rest of the corporate world, which has already created a set of weird terms and expressions. If you can master both sets, you have really expanded your overall job marketability.

# Drum up

## *What does this mean?*

Go get (as in new business, additional resources, or project support)

## *What this doesn't mean:*

We're starting a drum circle at work. Don't worry about knowing how to play the drums. No one else in the circle has any idea how to play either, except for Davis who is always gloating about how he used to be a professional timpanist in the New York Philharmonic before deciding to pursue an exciting career at the IT help desk. And Ken from Finance has no sense of rhythm anyway.

## *How is this used in a sentence?*

"We've almost hit our target for the year, but we're still three percent off our expected improvements from last year. We need to get out there and drum up some new business before the quarter closes."

## *More information:*

Unfortunately, drum line, marching band, or professional timpani experience in high school, college, or the New York Philharmonic won't help you here.

# Elephant in the room

### What does this mean?

There's a really big and blatantly obvious issue we are all ignoring because we don't want to, don't know how to, or can't deal with it.

### What this doesn't mean:

JoAnne wondered if she had just been working too hard and was hallucinating when she saw a giant circus elephant wearing Jim's tie sitting across the table from her.

### How is this used in a sentence?

"The real elephant in the room here is that our compensation strategy is completely misaligned with our corporate strategy for growth. We can continue making Band-Aid improvements, but nothing will change until we take a real look at our strategy, and no one in this room wishes to acknowledge that our strategy is outdated."

### More information:

Don't make the mistake of jumping right into trying to solve the elephant in the room problem. First, try to help everyone acknowledge the elephant. Many of your colleagues will still be in denial that the elephant even exists, let alone is in the room with you. If you can somehow convince everyone in the room that the elephant needs attention, *then* you might want to try to solve the problem together. Unfortunately, nine times out of ten, people in the conference room will not admit to seeing any trace of an elephant whatsoever. And while frustrating to those who see the elephant's reality, the conversation will typically shift to agenda topics more critical to the business, such as what should be served at the annual company recognition awards dinner.

*Note:* Sometimes, you may hear the expression "the dead moose on the table." While a bit more graphic, it is synonymous with "the elephant in the room." If you hear this, don't mistakenly assume that the leadership team is going on a hunting team building trip. Despite the fact that the two terms are essentially interchangeable, no one knows why the moose has to be dead and the elephant gets to live. Or whether a dead moose rotting on the table represents a bigger problem than an out-of-control live elephant trampling through the conference room.

*Elephant in the room*

*Dead moose on the table*

*Elevator speech*

# Elevator speech

### What does this mean?

The short verbal description of a project or program that hits on all of the key points and that can, for all intents and purposes, be delivered in a 30-second elevator ride

### What this doesn't mean:

Go make a speech on an elevator. Try the service elevator first. Those guys can't wait to hear your thoughts on our marketing plan for the next generation product.

### How is this used in a sentence?

"Before we really communicate this out to the rest of the organization, we should determine what our elevator speech is. That way, when we bump into people in the halls, we'll all be able to give them the same quick overview of what will be happening."

### More information:

The jury is out as to whether an elevator speech has ever taken place on an actual elevator. To get to the bottom of this important matter, I will be conducting an extensive study on the subject in hopes of publishing a powerful article about it in the next *Harvard Business Review*. Or maybe we should just accept that it has a better ring to it than the "bump-into-people-in-the-hallway speech" or the "bathroom speech."

The elevator speech is often intended for executives, who have little time for detailed descriptions of anything. But as everyone at all levels becomes busier and busier, thus requiring us to talk in sound bites, elevator speeches are becoming more important if you want to get any message across successfully.

# Flesh this out

### What does this mean?

Put some content on an outline and/or begin to create some detail

### What this doesn't mean:

Anything to do with flesh of any kind. We're not having a corporate barbecue.

The executives in the boardroom sat in collective stunned silence after viewing Mary's video outlining strategies on how to kill the competition. Beads of sweat started to roll down her forehead as she feared that she had gone astray by incorporating *Animal Planet* footage of lionesses in the Serengeti tearing apart and devouring the flesh of their prey.

### How is this used in a sentence?

"I think we've got a good start on this, but until we really flesh this out, we're not going to know if we have a new process that can be sustained by the organization."

### More information:

"Flesh this out" is related to a couple of other terms you might hear: "put some flesh on the bones" or "put some meat on the bones"—both also being rather graphic ways of saying that we need to put some content to an outline.

*Note:* This term is frequently confused with another expression in the corporate world—"flush this out"—meaning throwing metaphorical grenades at a project to expose and force out issues. I once overheard a surprisingly heated debate between two coworkers vehemently arguing about which was the right term to use in their speaking points. I was thrilled to see that they were focused on this very important debate, as opposed to the actual work, which was due first thing in the morning.

# Gain traction

## *What does this mean?*

Get buy-in, gain momentum

## *What this doesn't mean:*

John was concerned when he was urged by one of his closest friends on the leadership team to buy better tires for his car. He had heard about the CEO's idea for a new and seemingly misguided top talent program called "survival of the fittest" involving, among other draconian things, relocating the corporate office to the top of a large hill with only dirt road access. He had even heard the CEO emphatically proclaim, "If you can't even get to the office, you are not the type of leader we need here." But could this really be happening? And how would he compete in his economy electric car against all of those SUVs?

## *How is this used in a sentence?*

"This project is not gaining any traction with the key stakeholders. We seem to start and stop all the time. If we aren't able to really gain traction quickly, we may have to discontinue this work."

## *More information:*

At times, you will hear people referring to "spinning their wheels"—the notion that the tires are spinning fast but the vehicle is going nowhere—after mentioning that they are having difficulty gaining traction on a project or with key leaders. Using these two terms together is a very powerful way to elicit sympathy from others but still gets you no closer to improving the outcome.

# Gatekeeping

### What does this mean?

Closely protecting or blocking people from getting access to information, people, or a given area

### What this doesn't mean:

Everyone knew that Alan was fanatical about college football, but most thought it was overkill and just generally weird that as the head of security he had placed guard alligators at all access gates to the building as a proud tribute to his alma mater.

That old dilapidated gate in front of the Operations building is falling apart again. We need to get it fixed up. Maybe we can get some easy company publicity out there by appearing on one of those television DIY fixer-upper programs.

### How is this used in a sentence?

"I'm concerned that there is some gatekeeping going on with Nathan's team. He doesn't seem to be providing any of the information we need in a timely manner. If he were more accessible, we could help him understand that this new process won't threaten his current organization."

### More information:

Whereas keeping information contained is often necessary, frequently gatekeeping occurs when people feel threatened in some way by a current project or they view the information they have as giving them power in a dysfunctional corporate political dynamic. As such, gatekeeping is a common occurrence in the corporate world and can manifest itself at all levels—from administrative assistants to top leadership. Just know that wherever there is information, there is a diligent gatekeeper of that information, even if there is no guard alligator around.

# Get our arms around this

### What does this mean?

We need to get full understanding of what is going on.

### What this doesn't mean:

As Patti put her arms around her computer monitor, embracing it with all of the passion she usually saved for her husband after a long business trip, she wondered if she was being too literal in response to Eric's request that the team get its arms around this computer hardware issue.

### How is this used in a sentence?

"If we don't get our arms around this quickly, the entire project could be in jeopardy of missing critical timelines."

### More information:

Who is likely to say this? Anyone who feels as though something is not clear, defined, or under control, which describes about 93.4% of all things in the corporate world.

When you hear this term, understand that it is not meant to be interpreted as a progressive approach to team building and improving working relationships. Don't hug anyone. Just acknowledge that you agree that we really need to get our arms around this. Add that there are probably other important issues that we need to get our arms around as well, which will be true 100% of the time.

*Getting all of our ducks in a row*

# Getting all of our ducks in a row

### *What does this mean?*

We are prepared. Everyone and everything on the project, in the function, or in the department is lined up the way we want it: organized and planned.

### *What this doesn't mean:*

Janet thought she was making a strong statement of team alignment when she proudly lined up her extensive rubber ducky collection, leading directly into the executive boardroom. Unfortunately, and of no surprise to anyone who had witnessed her strange display, her credibility from that point forward was shot.

### *How is this used in a sentence?*

"We've got to have a team meeting so that we can make sure we've got all of our ducks in a row before we present this to the senior leadership team."

### *More information:*

This expression is often used on a project that is not proceeding exactly according to plan (assuming a plan exists). Usually, when one hears the "ducks in a row" expression, the team is experiencing an uncomfortable sense of being in some sort of disarray. This, of course, is disarray that has moved well beyond the usual level of disarray many of us have grown to expect and embrace on a day-to-day basis in the corporate world.

When trying to use this expression, please note that even though in nature many birds imprint and therefore follow each other in a row, in the corporate world, we are only allowed to reference *ducks* in a row. Substituting chickens, turkeys, or geese is not socially acceptable.

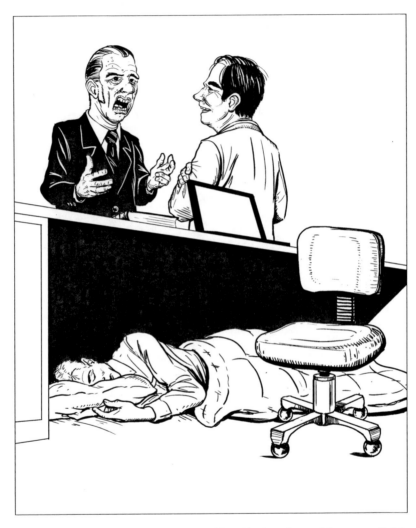

*After three sleepless nights working tirelessly on his greenfield project, Elliot fell asleep under his desk, hoping the right idea would finally come to him in his dreams.*

# Greenfield

### What does this mean?

Completely new with no history, guidelines, or constraints

### What this doesn't mean:

We're going golfing.

We'll be having our next executive retreat out in the middle of a field to get away from the static corporate environment. Walter from Human Resources came up with this progressive recommendation. Upon further reflection, though, we realize that we may not have fully thought this idea through. After watching Barry and Bill try to carry that conference table through the park, we've got a 75% chance that this is going to end up as a worker's compensation claim.

### How is this used in a sentence?

"This program is new. We have a rare opportunity with a greenfield. We can make it whatever we want."

### More information:

Greenfield projects can be a lot of fun because you have the opportunity to develop something from scratch. Unfortunately, that also means that no one in the company really has any idea whatsoever how to do it. Good luck.

*Harness the organic process*

# Harness the organic process

### What does this mean?

We are going to build on capabilities or competencies we currently have within the organization as opposed to acquiring them from the outside.

### What this doesn't mean:

As part of our wellness initiative, from this point forward, we are only going to be serving organic foods grown in the new garden that the top executive team planted. Unfortunately, so far the garden has only yielded three aphid-infested bok choy plants and one very oddly shaped squash that the CFO has expressed a desire to use as a paperweight on his desk.

Anything related to the medical marijuana industry

### How is this used in a sentence?

"Let's really harness the organic process here internally instead of bringing in outside talent who might not fit within our culture."

### More information:

There's not much more to say about an expression as ridiculous as "harness the organic process."

# Hit the ground running

### What does this mean?

Expecting a person, team, or project to be able to get started and be effective quickly or immediately without a lot of learning or ramp-up time

### What this doesn't mean:

As Tom carefully applied the icepack to his head, he finally conceded that he needed to stop setting up back-to-back meetings at opposite ends of the building. For the third time this week, while carelessly running through the hallways, he once again took a nasty nosedive, flipping over the copy machine on that infamous blind turn at the south end of the Customer Service department.

### How is this used in a sentence?

"Wilson really needs to hit the ground running when he gets on board because we've got some critical initiatives that need to move forward within the next 90 days."

### More information:

Running is the only way to hit the ground in the corporate world. Nobody will be described as "hitting the ground crawling," "hitting the ground speed walking," or even "hitting the ground jogging at a nice warm-up pace." Full speed is the only way to hit the ground in the fast-paced business world these days.

# Hit the nail on the head

*What does this mean?*

Exactly right

*What this doesn't mean:*

You hit a nail on its head, instead of your thumb like last time.

*How is this used in a sentence?*

"Mike really hit the nail on the head with his analysis of the limitations of our current quality systems."

*More information:*

Despite the allusion to carpentry or other home repair, you cannot substitute other tool-related expressions like "Nate, you really screwed that screw in perfectly."

*I'll ping you*

# I'll ping you

### What does this mean?

I'll e-mail you.

I'll send you a text message.

I'll IM (instant message) you.

### What this doesn't mean:

Due to the highly confidential nature of this potential acquisition, we'll be using Morse code from now on for all communications on this project.

We'll be watching the classic movie *The Hunt for Red October* as part of our latest training event to draw parallels between submarine communication patterns and our cross functional team dynamics.

### How is this used in a sentence?

"I'll ping you later so we can talk about the status of that project."

### More information:

Who is likely to say this? Leaders in the high-tech industries. Consultants who consult to leaders in the high-tech industries. Staff who work for leaders or consultants who work in the high-tech industries. People who like to sound like they work in high-tech industries. Anyone who has the latest smartphone and wants to sound cool.

Just make sure you check your e-mail or text messages (which shouldn't be a problem given that we are all compulsively obsessed with our cell phones).

# Increase the footprint

### What does this mean?

Increase our market share

Expand the work we are doing either in quantity or breadth

### What this doesn't mean:

Your shoe size has gotten bigger—not typical to see in a fully grown 43-year-old man, unless you are experiencing some unintended physical side effects from the illicit performance enhancing drugs Diane secretly gave you that promised to increase your spreadsheet processing power by 32% in time for the year-end incentive plan payout.

As a Bigfoot enthusiast, Walter from HR could hardly contain his excitement upon seeing the gigantic footprints traversing the corporate campus leading into the Payroll building. But how could he have missed the obvious for so long? Had Bigfoot really been hiding out as a payroll analyst under the employee alias of Sass Kwatch for the past six years? And how could Walter have allowed himself to be so consumed with merely correcting Kwatch's weekly payroll errors and not seeing the bigger picture regarding the huge and conspicuously hairy payroll analyst's true identity?

### How is this used in a sentence?

"If we are able to sell some add-on work to the current project, we'll really begin to increase our footprint with the client."

"We need to increase our footprint in the market, compared with our competitors, if we are going to be successful with this product line."

# Industry space

### *What does this mean?*
Industry

### *What this doesn't mean:*
Space, as in the "final frontier"

Anything that has to do with office space

### *How is this used in a sentence?*
"We really need to sell more work in the high-tech industry space."

### *More information:*
Just understand that whatever industry has had the word "space" added to it as a suffix is actually no different than the industry without this suffix.

Also note that one cannot merely add the word "space" to everything and expect a similar level of acceptance. Don't try mentioning something to the CFO about "budget space." He'll likely think you are talking about the cost of space planning and refer you to the Facilities department.

*Map this out*

# Map this out

### What does this mean?

Put a plan together or lay out a process graphically so everyone can see the start, progress to date, and the finish

### What this doesn't mean:

Open up your navigation app on your phone, and plot the fastest route from the corporate headquarters to your regional office in Tempe, Arizona.

Not fully understanding what the CIO meant when asking him to map out a solution to the company's software challenges, Larry beamed exuberantly, sensing an opportunity to apply everything he had learned in his recently completed cartography course.

### How is this used in a sentence?

"We need to map this out clearly so that we can develop an effective strategy and subsequent project plan."

### More information:

Often, mapping a process out involves many people in a room brainstorming while swarming around a whiteboard. Usually, one eager employee takes the lead by jumping up to grab a dry erase marker to depict graphically all that is being discussed during the brainstorming session. Frequently, another employee will jump up and take the marker out of the first employee's hand to write something new (or add to what is already depicted).

Sometimes the end results of these sessions are very clear and lead to effective next steps, a "roadmap" of sorts. Sometimes what gets depicted on the whiteboard is completely unintelligible to anyone who was not part of the process, let alone people who *were* part of the process, yielding a collective "what the hell did we mean by any of this?!" Unfortunately, the result is often the need to regroup and map it out again.

In this type of work, you may also hear the expressions "let's whiteboard this" or "we need to storyboard this." Both are synonymous with "map this out."

# Mindshare

### What does this mean?

Ideas coming from more than one person or from a group

### What this doesn't mean:

Bonnie is recommending some sort of Vulcan "mind-melding" activity at the next project brainstorming session. You might want to conveniently miss this one.

### How is this used in a sentence?

"We need to get some good mindshare going on this project. The situation is complex, and I want to make sure we are incorporating input from all of our team members on this one."

### More information:

Who is likely to say this? Consultants. Other employees in your company who are looking to generate ideas from many different sources. Coworkers who are only doing this dumb corporate job until their acting career takes off and they land a key role in the next *Star Trek* movie.

# On point

### What does this mean?

Good idea and one that is relevant to the current discussion

### What this doesn't mean:

Upon hearing his supervisor's words, Daniel—consumed mentally with his after-work activities—had thought he had heard the command "En pointe!" and eagerly rushed to lace up his pointe shoes for the ballet class that he and five of his manufacturing line buddies had been secretly taking after work. He was mortified but could only retreat quietly to his seat, hoping people would forget what they had seen here today.

### How is this used in a sentence?

"Nancy, that idea is right on point."

### More information:

If you are the person who is being lauded for being on point, take pride in the fact that you have successfully contributed to the conversation. Also recognize, however, that just because you made a comment that was on point, it doesn't mean that anything will come of this comment. Just be happy that you were verbally rewarded for making a constructive comment. Sadly, many on-point points have been buried in corporate bureaucracy.

*Note:* This term has bled far beyond the corporate world. Recently, a friend commented that my cooking of our Thanksgiving turkey was right on point. Whereas I was sad to hear this expression used to describe my cooking, he was right. That turkey was moist, well-seasoned, and generally phenomenal.

*Out of pocket*

# Out of pocket

### What does this mean?

You are not in the office or available that day or for that period of time.

### What this doesn't mean:

In an effort to make a bold leadership statement to his team, Will purposely wore pants with no pockets to prove that he had nothing to hide. His odd attempt at transparency had a lukewarm response with his team, who seemed more concerned with the new fashion statement he was making.

Anything at all related to pockets of any kind: pants pockets, Hot Pockets, the often elusive musical pocket (for any corporate musicians)

### How is this used in a sentence?

"Let Chris from Operations know that I'll be out of pocket for the next two days but can meet next week."

### More information:

The opposite of "out of pocket" is not "in pocket" (when you are trying to describe yourself as being in the office and available). Numerous unsuccessful attempts have been made to incorporate this as a usable expression. If you tell someone at work that you are in pocket, they will have absolutely no idea what you are talking about. I tried. Subsequent feedback suggested that I needed to work on my communication skills.

*Paradigm shift*

# Paradigm shift

### What does this mean?

A complete and significant change in approach, strategy, process, or culture (as opposed to a small incremental change)

### What this doesn't mean:

"Who let this guy start talking?!" Fred proclaimed with exasperation. "All I said was that we needed a paradigm shift, and suddenly the new R&D guy—some guy named Stephen Hawking—has been lecturing us for the last 40 minutes on quantum physics, something called a multiverse, and other weird stuff he calls quarks. No one knows what he's talking about, but we're getting way behind on our discussion about how to change our company culture."

### How is this used in a sentence?

"The only way we are really going to enact some change to this culture is to create a complete paradigm shift around how we work together, how we make decisions, and how we evaluate our risk tolerance in these new markets."

But probably not...

"I've got your paradigm shift right here."

"The paradigm isn't the only thing that needs shifting around here."

"Don't be shifting my paradigm. I'll shift my own paradigm when I'm good and ready."

### More information:

Who is likely to say this? Anyone wanting to sound strategic or confuse others so that what he or she is proposing sounds more strategic than it really is. Unfortunately, no one knows what a paradigm shift really looks like in the corporate world or, equally importantly, how to make one happen.

"We may uncover the root causes of this problem when we start to peel back the onion and find the underlying challenges."

# Peel back the onion

### What does this mean?

Discovering and uncovering layers of more pertinent information related to a project or a problem/issue that is being analyzed

### What this doesn't mean:

Everyone respected Alan for being a very sensitive manager. In fact, he seemed to be on the verge of tears when meeting with his employees after lunch to discuss some challenging company issues impacting them. It wasn't until Laura discovered that Alan had been secretly chopping onions in the company cafeteria at lunch time that he was exposed as an insensitive fraud.

### How is this used in a sentence?

"I think we are going to uncover the root causes of this problem when we start to peel back the onion and find out the underlying challenges the team has been facing."

### More information:

The expression refers to the additional layers of information uncovered at each subsequent layer of the onion. As such, you cannot reference peeling back other fruits or vegetables, even if those fruits have a peel. You could not say, "We need to peel back the orange on this one."

*Picking the low-hanging fruit*

# Picking the low-hanging fruit

### What does this mean?

Pursuing short-term goals that can be met relatively quickly and easily as part of a project. These quick achievements can help a project team gain important momentum.

### What this doesn't mean:

We're picking low-hanging fruit from the U-pick apple orchard tomorrow as a group team building exercise.

Anything at all that has to do with fruit, vegetables, or anything else in your grocery store's produce section

### How is this used in a sentence?

"Let's focus on picking the low-hanging fruit here first for the next few months before we go after the longer-term strategic project outcomes."

### More information:

You may also hear the expressions "quick wins" or "quick hits." Just to be clear, in the corporate world, "quick hits" does not refer to what a boxer does when effectively jabbing at his opponent with fast repetition. And "quick wins" does not refer to a team that puts away opponents in the first quarter and coasts the rest of the way to victory. "Picking the low-hanging fruit," "quick wins," and "quick hits" are all interchangeable. "Picking the low-hanging fruit" seems to be the term of choice, but this should not deter you from mixing it up from time to time. You don't want your terminology to get stale.

Despite these choices, understand that vegetables cannot ever be substituted for fruit, and kicks can never be substituted for hits. No one will understand you if you say "quick kicks" or "dig up the ripened vegetables." That would be weird. Because, of course, saying "picking the low-hanging fruit" *isn't* weird.

# Power alley

### What does this mean?

An area of strength, a competency or strong skill set, something that an employee is really good at

### What this doesn't mean:

The gap space in the baseball outfield between the center fielder and the left or right fielder where power hitters hit "gappers" for doubles and triples

### How is this used in a sentence?

"We should have Smith take on this project because it is really in his power alley."

### More information:

If someone is making reference to the fact that this is a power alley of yours, do not make the mistake of thinking that they are always giving you a compliment. Often, they are. Understand, though, that this may also be an attempt to flatter you into taking on work they do not want to do themselves—a common subversive corporate tactic. You must be careful, however, when refuting that this is truly not your power alley because you might still find yourself doing all of the work but now under the context of it being a "learning opportunity."

*Note:* You may also hear the term "bailiwick" used as a synonym for "power alley." Bailiwick? As a protest to this ridiculous word, I will spend no more time writing about it.

# Prepare a deck

### What does this mean?

Prepare a PowerPoint presentation

### What this doesn't mean:

We're working with Facilities on preparing and treating the deck in front of the new building for the upcoming rainy season. Go to Home Depot and take one of those crash courses on DIY home improvement.

Go get your rigged deck of cards. The senior executives have invited us to poker night, and this is our chance to make some money back after we got screwed on that annual incentive payout.

### How is this used in a sentence?

"I'll need you to prepare a deck for us to present at our meeting tomorrow afternoon with senior leadership."

### More information:

Who is likely to say this? Consultants. Company employees who used to be consultants. Company employees who have been hanging out a lot with consultants.

This expression originated before computer applications existed for making presentations. As such, the predecessor to these presentation applications was a series of photographic slides in a slide tray. When assembled into a presentation, the collection of slides was called a deck, as in a deck of cards. That being the case, no one is really sure how a PowerPoint presentation—which doesn't look remotely like a slide tray or a deck of cards—became known as a deck. Nevertheless, led by the torch-carrying consultants, who seem to use the expression in approximately 76.8% of meetings in which they participate, the expression has invaded the corporate world like the creature from the 1950s horror film *The Blob*.

When you hear this directed at you, just make sure you have good PowerPoint skills, and hopefully, you'll have more than 24 hours to put this deck together.

# Push back

### What does this mean?

Actively disagree (as opposed to passively disagreeing—the common act in the corporate world of nodding one's head in agreement and then proceeding to do anything but what was agreed to)

### What this doesn't mean:

When Mitch from Human Resources got out of his chair and shoved Ken from Finance, what had started as a verbal disagreement quickly devolved into a physical altercation with team members from both departments joining in a strange hockey-style bench-clearing brawl ironically taking place in the "Serenity Conference Room." When asked about the confrontation later, Mitch sheepishly responded, "Walter, my supervisor, told me at my last performance review that I needed to push back more. I was just trying to follow through on my development plan."

### How is this used in a sentence?

"I've got to push back on this one. I don't think that this is the best way for us to market this new product. We used a similar approach on the first generation product, and it didn't get us the market share we had anticipated."

### More information:

If you are the one pushing back, recognize that pushing back is a very effective approach for disagreeing in a politically correct way. Just be careful of how frequently you push back. If you push back too much, those who you are pushing against will begin to get tired of having push-back discussions about everything. They might even find creative ways to leave you out of the loop. If you see this happening, understand that you pushed back too frequently or too aggressively.

If you are the one being pushed back on, acknowledge your colleague's push back, and indicate that you love push back because it allows for great dialogue about all sides of an issue. You will be viewed as open-minded.

*Note:* Many in the corporate world are quite adept at pushing back strategically with the sole intention of creating a spiral of unresolved items and therefore precluding anything from getting done. They look like they are actively engaged but are really derailing progress to ensure that they don't have to do anything or change how they do things now. Just know who is pushing back on you, and determine whether the input is legitimate or merely a stall tactic.

# Put a stake in the ground

## *What does this mean?*

Taking a stand for what you believe, indicating that you won't budge beyond this point

## *What this doesn't mean:*

Go put a wooden stake in the ground in front of Stephanie's office, and tell her that you are gunning for her job. That'll really freak her out.

Dayle wasn't quite sure what to make of the strange invitation she received from the Procurement team asking her to join them for an exciting evening of vampire hunting after work. "These guys seem so normal at work," she thought as she contemplated the invitation. But she couldn't contain her morbid curiosity, which compelled her to meet them dressed in full Goth attire in the back parking lot once the sun went down.

## *How is this used in a sentence?*

"If we don't bring all three teams together for a meeting to understand our interdependencies, we're going to have problems downstream. I know you think we can do this over e-mail, but I've got to put a stake in the ground on this one. I think we really need to have everyone meet face-to-face to ensure we all end up on the same page."

## *More information:*

Putting a stake in the ground from time to time is a very effective way to drive home the point of how important your opinion is on a given subject. Don't make the mistake, however, of always threatening to put a stake in the ground. If you put too many stakes in the ground too frequently, your stakes become systematically less valuable each time. Eventually, your coworkers won't care *what* you do with your stake as long as you just stop talking, prompting your direct supervisor to coach you to "not die on this hill"—meaning in plain English, "Let it go! Please!! You're making us all look bad!"

# Road map

*What does this mean?*

A graphically depicted plan showing a destination or path

*What this doesn't mean:*

Get a road map out of the glove compartment of your car. For all of the Millennials, the road map was a map made out of a substance called paper that Baby Boomers and some Gen Xers used in the dark ages before cell phones, navigation apps, and GPS.

We'll be developing anything that looks even remotely like any road map you've ever seen. You will not find any actual roads on a corporate road map.

*How is this used in a sentence?*

"When we have finished mapping this out, we are going to need a road map that we can follow for the next 18 months during the critical implementation phase."

# Robust

### What does this mean?

Strong, well developed

### What this doesn't mean:

Strangely, this is a term that actually means what it means. There is something disturbing about that.

### How is this used in a sentence?

"We need to develop a robust talent acquisition program that will support current needs as well as our projected future growth."

### More information:

Prepare to hear this term excessively in the corporate world. Just know that if you can't describe it as robust, it's not good enough. In one full-day leadership meeting I attended, the term was used 42 times—eight times by one leader in a short five-minute pontification. Why I was immaturely tracking it, as opposed to listening to what he had to say, is another issue altogether.

# Scope creep

### What does this mean?

The project requirements that were initially agreed to have increased. Essentially, the scope we were responsible for delivering has crept up in size (usually without any additional resources, budget, or time to support the increase in work).

### What this doesn't mean:

Everyone on the project team had always thought the guy who developed the project scope had some very unsettling interpersonal mannerisms, but Lydia never suspected that the "Scope Creep" nickname she had jokingly given him would stick four years later.

### How is this used in a sentence?

"We need to be very careful that this doesn't turn into scope creep. We've only committed to these five project milestones within the next six to eight weeks. We can't add additional requirements because we don't have the ability to add additional resources, and we are on a fixed budget for this project."

### More information:

Don't be surprised that your project experiences scope creep. Almost every project ever conceived in the corporate world at some point runs into this phenomenon.

More importantly, you should be afraid. No need to scream dramatically, but definitely be afraid. Even though it is a regular occurrence, scope creep is often unchecked, leaving the project team with an unreasonable amount of additional work and no additional help. Some projects experience this more severely than others. Often, systems implementations suffer from the seemingly everyday occurrence of someone else attempting to slide new requirements into the project, even a mere week before launch. Just know that "creep happens."

*Sexy project*

# Sexy project

### What does this mean?

A very high profile and/or really interesting and cutting-edge project that can really advance an employee's career

### What this doesn't mean:

We've just landed an account with a top modeling agency. We think that the assessment phase of this project is critically important and that we really need to take a trip to the next beach photo shoot to interview all of the models extensively—we'll probably need to interview them multiple times at many different photo shoots just to make sure we have all of the necessary information. This could take months of diligent, painstaking research. It'll be hard, but we'll suffer through it.

Wow, this project has some really good looking people. Everyone wants in on this one, even though HR policy strictly prohibits coworker dating.

### How is this used in a sentence?

"Everyone wants to transfer into this business unit because all the sexy projects are here."

"I realize that this isn't the sexy project that you wanted to be working on, but the work you've been doing is critical."

### More information:

If you hear this term about a project, don't develop a list of project parts that you find especially sexy or those that just don't turn you on as much. Your coworkers may become slightly uncomfortable around you.

More importantly, try not to let the fact that your colleagues just referred to a *process reengineering project* as sexy make you feel confused about whether you've lost touch with reality.

*Darrin lost his appetite when his supervisor warned him, "If you aren't careful, Darrin, the organization won't see any value in your project, and it will become shelfware."*

# Shelfware

## What does this mean?

A document or project that has had extensive work performed on it but for a variety of reasons will never actually be implemented (no one to do it, doesn't work from a practical standpoint, changes in organizational direction). As a result, the project gets placed on someone's office bookshelf likely to never be opened again.

## What this doesn't mean:

We need to call Facilities to build new shelves in Conference Room B. Larry broke them when he tried to store the massive binders summarizing all 12 failed attempts to implement project Double Helix.

## How is this used in a sentence?

"If we're not careful, the organization won't see the project as having any value, and it will become shelfware."

## More information:

Who is likely to say this? Project team members or consultants who are sensing that the project on which they are working is not receiving strong support within the organization and from important leaders.

If possible, try to stay as far away from this project as possible. Inevitably, you will put in a lot of hours for a project outcome that will never be implemented. On the positive side, at least you will have participated in the generation of numerous very aesthetically pleasing PowerPoint presentations.

*Singing from the same song sheet*

# Singing from the same song sheet

### What does this mean?

Not only does everyone on a project or team know and understand what we are doing, but we are all telling the same story to everyone else about what we're doing—even when subjected to interrogation-like grilling from senior executives.

### What this doesn't mean:

We'll be singing from a song sheet for our report out to the executives next week. We know that this is a very nontraditional approach, but we have intel that our new CIO has an affinity for Broadway musicals. Before joining our company, he had apparently performed in several off-Broadway renditions of *Cats* and *The Phantom of the Opera*. We think this approach will help us get the green light.

Several employees from the IT, Operations, and Legal departments are forming a band to perform at the next employee town hall meeting. Lead singer needed. Auditions will take place in Conference Room C on the fourth floor today starting at 5:00 p.m. Load all equipment through the service elevator.

### How is this used in a sentence?

"Before we go into this meeting, let's make sure we are all singing from the same song sheet so that we don't look like we're not aligned."

### More information:

Who is likely to say this? Anyone on any project that isn't going well. Usually when the "singing from the same song sheet" expression emerges, someone is trying desperately (but often unsuccessfully) to get everyone moving in the same direction in a coordinated manner.

Sometimes, the "singing from the same song sheet" statement is followed by an exasperated comment that getting everyone aligned is like "trying to herd cats."

*Socialize the plan*

# Socialize the plan

### What does this mean?

We need to go to all of the key people likely to be impacted by what we are doing to make sure they buy into it, endorse it, and/or sponsor it.

### What this doesn't mean:

What started as a simple attempt to have a few drinks and spend more social time together after work as a cross functional project team quickly escalated when Denise began to run around the Data Center with a lamp shade on her head. Everyone breathed a collective sigh of relief that Judy from Legal had gone home early.

### How is this used in a sentence?

"Let's socialize this plan and these changes with the rest of the organization to ensure that they get implemented quickly."

### More information:

Understand that socializing the plan in the corporate world has nothing to do with socializing as we would in the normal world. In the corporate world, somehow we socialize concepts, philosophies, projects, and changes. And if you work in a consensus-driven culture—meaning that everyone needs to agree about any and all action items before anyone is allowed to do anything—you may find yourself spending significantly more time socializing your plan than the plan required to develop in the first place.

*"I'll be back in the office on Friday. Let's talk live then."*

# Talk live

### What does this mean?

A conversation where we use our actual voices and forego our continuously evolving reliance on e-mail, text messages, or instant messaging

### What this doesn't mean:

Today on *Business Talk Live*, we bring you riveting coverage of our ongoing hard-hitting series "A Day in the Life of Our Employees." In this highly anticipated segment, we will be providing coverage of a meeting between Gene from Procurement and Gloria from Legal. The topic for the meeting: the benefits administration outsourcing vendor contract review. Please be aware that what you are about to witness is totally live and will not be edited for content, despite the history of explosive interpersonal dynamics we have seen between these two in previous contract review sessions.

### How is this used in a sentence?

"I'll be back in the office on Friday. Let's talk live then."

### More information:

There is no antonym to talking live (as in "talk dead"); however, years ago an employee, who for his own safety has asked that his identity and company remain anonymous, found himself trapped in a conference room for three hours while another project team monotonously read verbatim from their 247-slide PowerPoint presentation. It is rumored that several members of the audience needed resuscitation. Urban legend has it that the expression "death by PowerPoint" was born in that very meeting. Unfortunately, almost everyone in the corporate world has at one point or another almost perished at the hand of another's droning PowerPoint presentation delivery.

*Talking at the 20,000-foot level*

# Talking at the 20,000-foot level

### What does this mean?

Speaking or presenting about something at a very high strategic level only—without details

### What this doesn't mean:

Cathy emphatically announced to the team, "We've had enough of that contrived 'trust fall' team building exercise. We're taking this up a notch with a skydiving trip to improve our team's overall risk tolerance and performance. Lowest team performer goes without a parachute." Mike was suddenly concerned that his recent decision to slack off at work might have very dire consequences for him.

### How is this used in a sentence?

"I've only got knowledge of this at the 20,000-foot level, but it seems like the right direction for us to be moving and the correct strategy for us to take."

### More information:

Who is likely to say this? Executives. Leaders of any kind. Consulting firms that specialize in strategy and therefore want no part of anything having to do with real details or day-to-day business operations.

Usually, people who fashion themselves as highly strategic talk at the 20,000-foot level and, more importantly, tell you that they talk at the 20,000-foot level. Be careful when working with these people because:

- Frequently, the more strategic someone professes to be, the less strategic he or she really is.

- These people inevitably will not want to have anything to do with any details of any kind and typically consider themselves to be too strategic to have to spend time in the details. Just be very careful around 20,000-foot talkers. They'll talk a really good game, but they will do no work whatsoever and will be nowhere remotely close to anyone trying to implement the strategy they developed at the 20,000-foot level.

*"Let's tee this up at the next staff meeting to see if we can move forward with it in the next quarter."*

# Tee up

### What does this mean?

To present an idea for a decision

### What this doesn't mean:

We're going golfing. Tee up is not a synonym for tee time.

### How is this used in a sentence?

"Let's make sure we tee this up at the next staff meeting to see if we can move forward with it in the next quarter."

### More information:

When you hear this expression, don't get excited, drive home, and put on your audaciously ugly new golf pants, expecting the afternoon off for quality golfing and boondoggling time with your management team. But also don't get too far into the details of a project that is being teed up. If it is being teed up, it can also be shot down...and frequently is.

*Think outside the box*

# Think outside the box

### What does this mean?

Think creatively to come up with new and innovative solutions or ideas

### What this doesn't mean:

After four hours of sitting next to a large empty cardboard box recovered from the Shipping department, Carl became concerned that he still hadn't come up with any groundbreaking ideas.

### How is this used in a sentence?

"We really need to think outside the box on this one. The same old recycled solutions are going to get us nowhere on this."

But not...

"I'm so outside the box, I can't even see the box from where I'm standing."

### More information:

Who is likely to say this? Consultants who are paid to think outside the box. Anyone who already thinks that he or she is an out-of-the-box thinker and therefore more creative and innovative than everyone else.

"Think outside the box" is a classic expression that has been overused to the point of losing some of the inspirational luster that it may have once had. But it is still a staple term in the corporate world that is used frequently.

# Thoughtware

### What does this mean?

Creative or new ideas

### What this doesn't mean:

At first, Valerie was excited about the idea Tom had just presented. Unfortunately, her excitement quickly faded. She watched in horror as Tom proceeded to remove and open an empty Tupperware container from his desk, tilt his head towards it as if to let the idea fall out of his head into the container, and then close it with a pleased look as though he had just preserved a brilliant idea. If this was going to be her new boss, Valerie was now convinced that she had no choice but to resign first thing in the morning.

### How is this used in a sentence?

"We've got some good thoughtware here from the different regions on how to execute this strategy."

### More information:

Who is likely to say this? People who think using the simple word "ideas" makes them sound less intelligent than using the term "thoughtware." Research has proven that it has the opposite effect.

More importantly, however, don't try using the expression "ideaware." It is not an acceptable substitute. Nor is "conceptware" or "paradigmware." In addition, whereas many brainstorming sessions are facilitated with the notion that there are no bad ideas, some thoughtware just isn't very good. In these situations, you might hear someone allude to something called "vaporware," which refers to a really bad idea that is going nowhere—as in vaporizing into thin air. Just know that "vaporware" does not refer to the unspoken understanding that no one should sit next to Harold during lunch meetings when he has brought his now infamous homemade seven-bean salad.

# Tissue rejection

## *What does this mean?*

The organization will reject the new strategy, project, program, or process because it represents too much change too fast or violates a belief system.

## *What this doesn't mean:*

Anything at all to do with actual organ transplants

Nobody likes the scented tissues in the downstairs bathroom. Someone should mention to Purchasing that they should stick with the unscented variety next time.

## *How is this used in a sentence?*

"If we're not careful to talk with all of the key stakeholders and gain their buy-in, we could end up with tissue rejection of the new program we are looking to implement as a key component of this project."

## *More information:*

This expression is derived from a body rejecting an organ transplant, although it is still a mystery how or why it crept into corporate conversations from its true medical origins. To avoid any misunderstandings, employees working in health care should really think twice before using this expression when talking about anything other than surgery.

If you hear this lobbed in your general direction, just nod your head, agree, and try not to look confused about how the term "tissue rejection" ended up in your conversation about improvements in the annual operating budget planning process.

# Touch base

### What does this mean?

Talk or get in contact

### What this doesn't mean:

We're putting together our softball team for the annual company picnic, and we're looking for good base runners. Last year, Max from R&D was so slow that he was thrown out from right field while running to first on what would have been a single for anyone else. We haven't stopped hearing about it since.

### How is this used in a sentence?

"Let's touch base later this week to evaluate whether the team has been able to find some potential solutions to these problems."

### More information:

Touching base in general is important to people in the corporate world. When all else fails, just tell someone that you think you should touch base to continue discussing the subject at hand. Touching base generally makes people feel good, even if you are no closer to any resolution on anything. Also recognize that the statement "let's touch base *later*" is often merely an attempt to procrastinate. Most of the time, when someone wants to touch base later, he or she really just doesn't want to think about the problem at the current moment. In cases like this, just let him or her know that you'd be happy to touch base later. Everyone will be happy. Nothing will be solved. This might actually get you promoted.

# Turnkey solution

### What does this mean?

A solution to a problem within the organization that is simple and immediate

### What this doesn't mean:

After desperately chasing clues around the corporate campus for the better part of the morning, Brent finally arrived at the destination Larson had told him to find—a door he had never encountered before, behind which Larson had assured him were critical secret documents that would help him solve his project challenges. With hope, he turned the key, but his anticipation quickly turned to fury as he walked into the stinking and still partially flooded old executive washroom. He now knew that he had been duped with a practical joke and would be humiliated and still without solutions at that afternoon's business project review leadership meeting.

### How is this used in a sentence?

"This project isn't going to lend itself to a turnkey solution. A lot of integration and time will be required before we can stop the bleeding and improve our profit margins on this product."

### More information:

You may hear terms such as "flipping on the light switch" or "magic bullet" as well. These terms are related to "turnkey solution" but don't mean the exact same thing. Employees will refer to desired simple solutions that are as easy as flipping on a light switch. When you hear this, first realize that nothing in the corporate world is ever as easy as just flipping a switch. And second, don't get up from your seat in the middle of the CFO's PowerPoint presentation about the company's financial health to go turn on the lights.

Additionally, leaders will also refer to "magic bullets" when referencing the fact that there isn't any easy, perfect solution for this problem. Again, if you hear this, know that you are not going to be treated to a magic show today, other than your meeting with Jane from Finance who is a magician of sorts at somehow getting your department's budget under control.

# Value add

### What does this mean?

Recommendations that improve a process, structure, or business operations. Essentially, the recommendations or work are valuable to the organization.

### What this doesn't mean:

The term "value add" is not meant to be confused with the "value ad" (as in advertisement) that you take to the grocery store to ensure you save 99 cents on strawberries this week.

### How is this used in a sentence?

"We need to determine what our value add is. If we're not able to demonstrate that our methodology actually adds value, this whole initiative may be canceled."

### More information:

Given how prevalent this expression has become, you may frequently hear many derivations of it, such as "value proposition," "value creation," or "add value." Just know that they all essentially mean the same thing.

# Vectoring towards success

### What does this mean?

We are moving rapidly towards a successful project outcome.

### What this doesn't mean:

For some reason, the IT department has decided to incorporate dialogue from *Battlestar Galactica* into their daily team status meetings. Next week, we heard that they are going to talk like pirates all week on the IT help line. I think these developments may answer the question about whether we need new management in that department.

### How is this used in a sentence?

"If we keep up this good work on this project, we'll be vectoring towards success in achieving our strategy."

### More information:

Who is likely to say this? People nobody really wants to hang out with anyway.

# Walking the halls

## *What does this mean?*

The process by which consultants actively look for more project work from inside a current client by trying to meet with as many leaders as possible, whether related or unrelated to the current project scope

## *What this doesn't mean:*

Craig was frustrated that Warren never had to take on any additional project work, even though everyone else on the team was doing their share to pitch in. He was convinced that Warren had developed a devious plan to fool the project leader about how busy he was by regularly asking to leave team meetings early due to "competing priorities," only to walk for hours through the company halls with his laptop, a notepad, and a contemplative look on his face. But Craig couldn't prove anything.

## *How is this used in a sentence?*

"We don't really have a role for another manager on this project due to current project budget constraints, but we really need to get Floyd on a project. We could have him walk the halls at the client to see if he can sell some more work."

## *More information:*

Who is likely to say this? Consultants already working for a company on various projects but looking to generate more business and staff more consultants on more projects.

If you work for the consulting firm and are assigned the task of walking the halls, recognize the following:

- You have no real project assignments.
- You have no real input into the project team currently working at the client.
- You probably have little to no clout of any kind with the client.

Given those parameters, go sell some work quickly.

If you work for the client and overhear that someone is roaming the halls, don't panic. Just look for the consultant roaming around the place who looks like a poorly disguised secret agent sent on a reconnaissance mission. This individual will be fairly easy to spot as he or she will be trying to find a way to talk with you about "new opportunities" for projects. Engage at your own risk.

# War room

## What does this mean?

A room set aside as a temporary workspace for a critical project, where all resources and project team members are colocated for as long as the project exists

## What this doesn't mean:

Take us to DEFCON 1.

## How is this used in a sentence?

"Given how important this project is to our ability to penetrate this new market, we need to create a war room where we can get all of our resources together to develop our strategies and approaches."

## More information:

Usually a war room is created with the intent to wallpaper the war room with road maps, strategies, plans, and approaches for the project. Typically, by the time the war room is complete, almost all walls are covered with diagrams, road maps, and butcher paper of some kind or another. It can either be aesthetically pleasing or cause complete information overload leading to an epileptic seizure.

All of the following will at some point or another occur in the war room (sometimes at the same time):

- Brainstorming sessions
- Concept mapping
- Road map creation
- Project planning
- 20,000-foot-level discussions
- Drilling down ...a lot...with many resulting headaches
- Straw men building...and straw men killing
- Ideas teeing up, ideas being shot down
- PowerPoint preparation, PowerPoint editing, PowerPoint editing again...and again...and again

- PowerPoint e-mailing among war room residents while literally sitting two feet away from each other

Initially, seven people sitting in a confined conference room will seem like a lot of fun and an energetic environment to exchange ideas and get a lot done. Ultimately over time, you will find it more and more annoying to not have any privacy or leg room and to know intimately the strange eating habits and diet of Harold, your new war room buddy.

*Wear multiple hats*

# Wear multiple hats

### What does this mean?

Serving in more than one role on a project or in a function

### What this doesn't mean:

The vice president of R&D looked sternly and quizzically as Keith walked into the project meeting wearing his 50th anniversary Mickey Mouse ears, given to him at the last team building trip to Disneyland, on top of his New York Yankees baseball cap. Suddenly, Keith worried that he may have grossly misunderstood the memo from senior leadership stating that everyone should be ready to wear multiple hats.

### How is this used in a sentence?

"This job is going to require that the employee wear multiple hats at different times. We need to make sure that we get a person who has enough breadth of experience in a lot of different areas to ensure that he or she will be successful."

### More information:

Who is likely to say this? Anyone in the corporate world who feels as though they are understaffed—in other words, almost everyone in the corporate world.

Wearing multiple hats has essentially become a fundamental expectation. Rarely can an employee get by today utilizing a single skill set. In many ways, the need for employees to wear multiple hats is really code for "we don't have the budget for the right level of staff to get this done." That being the case, get ready to wear a lot of hats, as long as your Mickey Mouse ears stay at home.

# Where the rubber meets the road

### What does this mean?

Where theory turns into practice, things get real, and we find out if our new plan, program, process, or initiative actually works. We are no longer just marveling at our pretty PowerPoint presentations.

### What this doesn't mean:

Rubber, this is the road. Road, this is rubber. (My editor attempted to have this pathetically feeble attempt at a joke deleted three times. But an expression as bad as "where the rubber meets the road" deserves a joke as bad as this.)

### How is this used in a sentence?

"Until now, we have had no real data to support our theories. This is where the rubber meets the road—when we will test if this system actually works as anticipated."

### More information:

Unfortunately, very often when the rubber meets the road, all hell breaks loose because the theories presented in the beautifully artistic PowerPoint presentations were often created without the input of the people actually working in the company's operational areas. Just know that when the rubber meets the road, the journey will be bumpy, no matter how plush the car seats are.

# Win-win proposition

### What does this mean?

A solution that benefits and satisfies both parties in a negotiation

### What this doesn't mean:

Joe couldn't figure out why the new COO intimidated him so much, but he found himself unable to present his operations plan without stuttering nervously.

### How is this used in a sentence?

"We really need to stop looking at this problem as a situation where one side gains and the other loses. If we work together, we can create a win-win proposition."

### More information:

The "win-win proposition" is a very popular term in the corporate world. Given our growing levels of attention deficit disorder and our obsessive and frantic need to shorten terms due to a general lack of time (and as an attempt to sound cool), sometimes it will be shortened to just "win-win."

If you are involved in a discussion that gets resolved with a win-win proposition, you will be well regarded in the company for being able to develop creative solutions in a way that builds solid working relationships. Unfortunately, win-win propositions actually happen less frequently than they are discussed.

# Work thread

### What does this mean?

A section or subset of a project with assigned team members focused on that area

### What this doesn't mean:

This project has something to do with sewing.

### How is this used in a sentence?

"Let's get everyone in the Project Management office together to identify all of the critical work threads for this project. Then we can determine who should lead each work thread."

### More information:

Presumably, a "work thread" alludes to threads weaving together to create a bigger tapestry (or something like that). The same could apply to a synonymous expression "work stream," where small streams join together to make a large and powerful river of progress. All of it seems a bit too transcendental to me (although I have to admit that I have no idea what transcendental means).

Just know that the bigger the project, the more work threads. The more work threads, the more chance for confusion about whose work thread is doing what.

# A Final Note

Is there a point to this blatant lampooning of our corporate terminology? Aside from an effort to lighten up our view of our corporate selves and bring a little fun to the workplace, the real question being asked in this book is quite simply, "If we stop using these terms and instead speak in plain language, will we be better off?" The language we use every day certainly affects our motivation, engagement, productivity, achievements, and even our perceived credibility. So what happens to our work when we overuse all of these weird expressions? Will people take us less seriously as leaders if we continuously tell them that we need to be "singing from the same song sheet" or "create a paradigm shift"?

Although I'm certainly not aware of any complex algorithm that shows a statistically significant causal relationship between being written off as a leader and using expressions like these and others, in my experiences in leadership roles and consulting, I have noticed two impacts when these terms are hurled around with reckless abandon. Firstly, there's a lot of head scratching by those who just don't understand what is being said. Many of them probably aren't saying anything about their confusion based on a simple insecurity that drives them to wonder if maybe they are supposed to know what these things mean. I certainly wasn't publicizing to anyone earlier in my career when I had no idea what was being said. We all, of course, figure it out sooner or later. But why put ourselves through that? Figuring out how to navigate corporate politics and culture is hard enough without throwing a language barrier into the gauntlet. Secondly, and maybe more importantly, the credibility of the person using the terms can be damaged because his or her language feels inauthentic and doesn't connect or resonate with people—even if the speaker has something very valuable to say, which is often the case. The confounded head scratching is fairly straightforward and probably doesn't require any sort of highly advanced degree in industrial psychology to understand. But for the issue of credibility, I'll share a few of my past experiences.

The first experience occurred early in my career when I worked for a large global consulting firm. We had some really smart people working there who were really good at helping clients with some really hard problems. Yet many clients asked me—only somewhat jokingly—why we all talked so strangely. The consulting industry's sometimes nonsensical speech even spurred a comical "Consultese Bingo" game where clients would theoretically use bingo cards covered with our weird expressions and compete to fill their cards based on the different expressions they heard their consultants use every day. Even though we were doing some important and valuable work for the clients, we were also being laughed at in some circles behind the scenes. Were we written off as having no credibility? Definitely not. On the other hand, did we truly connect well with our clients in an authentic way? Maybe there was room for improvement there that might have had an effect on the value of the work we were doing with them.

The second experience occurred when I was working with a senior vice president within a multi-billion-dollar technology organization with more than forty thousand employees across the world. During a leadership team meeting, one of his vice presidents leaned over to me and whispered, "What we all like about you is that you translate what she says for us so we know what to do." Job security as a corporate translator aside, even though the senior vice president was an incredibly intelligent leader who was well versed in the organization's business challenges and had great insights and long-term strategies, she wasn't reaching her team of vice presidents and had completely lost the hundreds of employees who reported up through her departments. One year later, she exited the company with many of her strategies unfulfilled.

The third experience occurred when I had the chance to work with a chief operating officer for a mid-sized organization going through a critical transformational period. He was well known for beginning each of the global town hall webinars by saying, "Our job is simple: Make good stuff that people want to pay for. Then go sell that good stuff." Whereas he may have swung the pendulum far to the other side of the language continuum, when this leader spoke, he had all of our attention, and no one contended that they couldn't understand the message he was trying to communicate. He was one of the top executives in the company but was resonating as a regular guy. How did that help the organization? He was quoted a lot. People felt connected to him. They worked hard for him and for the company.

So what's my point? Let's try to talk to each other at work the way we would talk to our friends or family. Will it improve our performance and help our messages resonate better with our teams and co-workers? It's worth a try. At the very least, it would be an interesting case study.

*Heard any other ridiculous corporate expressions? We'd love to hear from you as we compile volume two! Join the conversation and reach us at www.jamessudakow.com.*

*The author and illustrator discuss thoughtware for their paradigm-shifting book.*

## About the Author

When he's not busy writing about the corporate world's frequently comedic dysfunction, James Sudakow serves as the principal of CH Consulting, Inc., a boutique management and organizational effectiveness consulting practice he founded in 2010. He specializes not only in refraining from using any of the expressions referenced in this book but also in helping companies manage organizational transformation and create talent management strategies and programs that maximize employee capabilities and improve business performance. Before starting his own consultancy, James held leadership roles in several global multibillion-dollar organizations across the technology and health-care industries. James currently lives in Southern California with his wife and three children, as well as the family's two rabbits and one lovably neurotic dog whose breed origins are a mystery to everyone in the family and will continue to be the subject of lively family debates until someone forks over the $80 required to get that DNA test at the next trip to the vet. James can be contacted at www.jamessudakow.com.

## About the Illustrator

Todd Kale began drawing with crayons as a child in Maryland. He has learned a little since then as the illustrations in this book were created with both traditional and digital media. His work has appeared in books, video games, film, and advertising. When a number of his clients started speaking the same cryptic phrases, he enlisted the help of his friend James Sudakow to translate the strange corporate dialect that had spread into the creative field. Todd's work is at www.toddkale.com.